THE ART OF THE RACE

by Amanda Lockhart

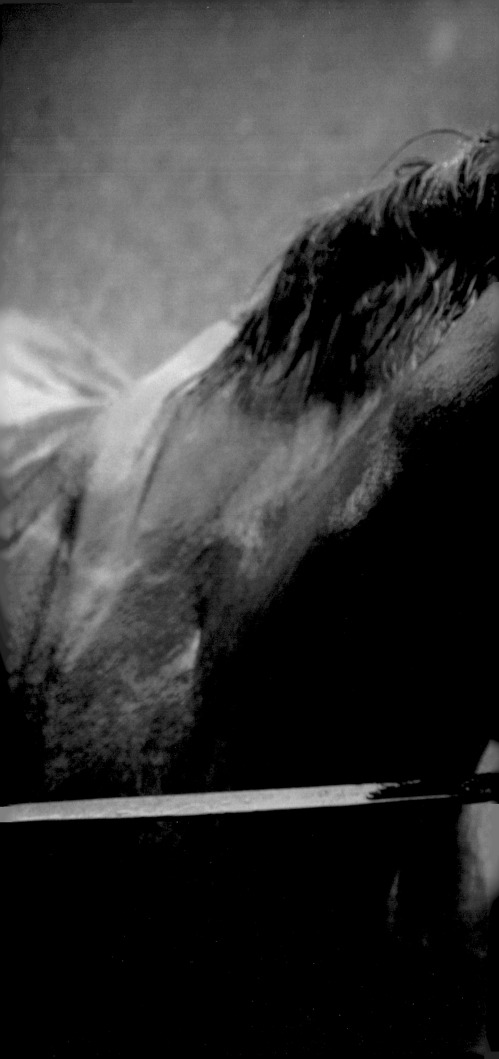

THE ART
OF THE RACE

CONTENTS

FOREWORD by Amanda Lockhart

I am indebted to everybody who has helped me during the making of this book. There are two people in particular without whom it would never have seen the light of day. The first is John Maxse, who tracked me down in the first place after seeing my hunting book, The Art of the Chase, and asked me if I would like to get involved in a project on racing under the aegis of the Jockey Club, for whom he was then working. He has worked tirelessly over the last few years to get me access behind the scenes of racing, to introduce me to people and to explain to me, sometimes with frustrating repetition and extreme patience, who was who (people and horses alike) and when and where I needed to be photographing things. The other is my husband, Ian Marris, for his unflinching support, encouragement and generosity.

I would also like to thank Sir Mark Prescott for agreeing to write the introduction, Dan Abraham for allowing me to use some of his fabulous images (credits on page 168) and the following people and organisations for allowing me to come and take pictures and to use them in this book:

The Jockey Club	Michael Bell
The National Stud	Henry Daly
Coolmore	John Gosden
Shadwell	Nicky Henderson
Juddmonte Farms	Philip Hobbs
Tweenhills Farm and Stud	Alan King
Newsells Stud	Charlie Mann
Silfield Bloodstock	Ginger McCain
The Racing School, Newmarket	Ferdy Murphy
Allertons	Martin and David Pipe
Berney's Saddlery	Oliver Sherwood

I am also enormously grateful to all of the other race photographers for all their help and advice and for putting me on the right track (sometimes literally) and to all the starters, especially Sean McDonald, for ferrying me about.

The Art of the Race is dedicated to my uncle, the late Dave Dick,
on whose name I have shamelessly traded during the making of
this book. Apart from being a much-missed family member, he
was one of Britain's best-loved jockeys, winner of one of the most
dramatic races of all time, the 1956 Grand National on ESB,
as well as the 1952 Cheltenham Gold Cup (and 346 other jump
races besides).

INTRODUCTION by Sir Mark Prescott

Having greatly enjoyed the photographs of hunting contained in Amanda Lockhart's first book, *The Art of the Chase*, I awaited her book of racing photographs, to be entitled *The Art of the Race*, with real anticipation. Consequently, I felt greatly privileged when asked to pen the book's introduction.

I may not have picked up the hunting book for a couple years, but many of its images are still engraved in my mind. I am sure the same will apply for many readers of this splendid book, which employs an artist's eye to portray the contemporary horseracing scene in photographs.

Interestingly, *The Art of the Chase* came out in 2005, at a most difficult time for hunting, for it was the height of the furore over the projected hunting ban. Nevertheless, the book far exceeded projected sales figures.

Now *The Art of the Race* arrives in the shops just as racing faces its own well-documented financial challenges from the effects of the recession and changes to the nature of the sport's grass-roots support. More particularly, it is being challenged by a dramatic fall in its central funding as a consequence of, among other things, the betting industry moving its operations off-shore.

Hunting has to a degree survived the legislators, and no doubt racing will manage to follow suit. However, once again, at a crucial time, Amanda Lockhart's photographs divert us from political controversy. Instead, she draws our eyes back to the essence of the sport concerned, and especially to that which matters most in the Sport of Kings - and yet which at times seems to be considered least – the horse.

For, clever though all of us horsemen may consider ourselves to be, the timeless attraction of the horse remains undimmed. Rather refreshingly, it also remains largely disdainful of our efforts to improve its performance by scientific means.

To illustrate the point, it is worth considering that Roger Bannister's first sub-four-minute mile has been broken thousands of times since his epic run in 1954. However, during that time, both the Derby and the Grand National's course records have fallen only three times each. This has happened despite the best scientific brains that money can buy attempting to improve racehorse performance with the advent of balanced diets, artificial gallops, treadmills, swimming pools, walking machines, bone scans, blood tests and endoscopy.

Amanda Lockhart's beautifully composed photographs, greatly aided by Dan Abraham's perfectly timed action shots, detail the great variety that comprises the racing scene in Britain and Ireland today. Ask any foreign racehorse owner what it is about racing here that attracts them most and entices them away from their far better endowed races at home, and the answer will almost certainly be that it is the racing public's affection for the horse, and the wide variety of our courses and training facilities, that draws them to our shores.

*

For several years, it was my good fortune to train for one of America's foremost owners, Mrs. Josephine Abercrombie. The only child of Jim Abercrombie, who had amassed a fortune in the Texas oil fields, she enjoyed an idyllic childhood and swept the board on her ponies at Madison Square Gardens.

In adult life she was seldom out of the headlines. She was married six times – to five husbands – without finding success. At various times she also managed a successful string of professional boxers ('Oh, Boxers – such lovely dogs I always think,' observed the late Queen Mother famously, when being appraised of Mrs. Abercrombie's interest). In addition, she trained racehorses herself on 'the backstretch' and founded the world-renowned Pin Oak Stud in Kentucky.

Even when approaching her 70s, Mrs. Abercrombie retained her startling good looks, her razor-sharp mind and her complete understanding of horses and racing. She attended Royal Ascot annually and stayed on for the week following the Royal meeting to see her horses in training in Europe. Once this pattern was established, it did not take me too long to appreciate that the post-Ascot week was the week of the year that mattered most.

During the last season that she had horses in training in Europe, our stable produced five of her seven horses to run nine times in the week in question. They won six races and were placed twice, including a second at the Royal Meeting. Mrs. Abercrombie attended all these races in person, zipping across the country in her private jet and picking up trophies as she went.

However, it was the historic, long-distance Cesarewitch Handicap, run at Newmarket in the autumn, that really perplexed and excited her. We had the hot ante-post favourite for the race, Hasten To Add (who was destined to finish fourth) and I rang her in advance to explain the intricacies of the race, and why I thought we should run.

"How far is the race?" she asked (few races in the USA being over more than 1½miles).
"Two miles and two furlongs," I ventured.
"How many runners will there be?" (12 being the maximum at most tracks in the States).
"Thirty six," I answered.

"And how many times do they go round the track for goodness' sake?" she queried, sounding increasingly incredulous.

"There's only one ninety-degree turn," I replied, feeling that I was probably losing ground.

"You must be mad!" she concluded.

Despite her reservations, she came over for the great day. She was so excited at the prospect of the race that she was noted prowling about with her hat on fully two hours before we were due to leave for the races.

Gazing across the vast expanse of Newmarket Heath, the runners at the start for the Cesarewitch far out of sight, she was asked at this moment of tension, by the senior steward, what she thought of it all.

"Gee, it sure is something special – to be surrounded by all these Dooks and Duchesses staring into the distance looking at nothing," came the legendary reply.

*

Like so many people destined to become an aficionado of the bullfight, my initial interest in the corrida was stimulated first by the black and white photographs (and not the rather laboured prose and contrived text) of Ernest Hemingway's book *Death in the Afternoon*. Subsequently, my first visit to a corrida at Pamplona was initiated by reading the same author's *The Sun Also Rises*.

Aged 16, too young to drive and plastered with acne, I had just left school, ridden a couple of winners and acquired my first girlfriend. As she was two years older (a lifetime at that age), I had felt compelled to lie about my age. When asked where we should go for a week's holiday in July, the lack of a driver's licence promised to expose my deceit. "We'll go to Pamplona," I heard myself say.

I barely knew where Pamplona was and certainly had no idea how to get there. Three days' travel, by three different coaches, saw us arrive exhausted. Also, Mr. Hemingway had failed to make it sufficiently clear to me that the 20,000-strong population of Pamplona swelled to 250,000 during the festival of San Fermín.

Far from the cosy bed and breakfast accommodation that I had envisaged, we found ourselves forced to sleep on the steps of the Council Offices. Mercifully, after three days of discomfort and frustration, an entrepreneurial Spanish landlady, alerted to our plight and sensing a good business opportunity, allowed us to take over a double room from 9am to 3pm. It was vacated each day during those hours by an elderly American couple, who were researching gothic churches and were horrified to find themselves surrounded by a quarter of a million drunks all night and six bulls hurtling along the street each morning.

Amongst a maelstrom of new emotions, experiences and ultimately stimulating memories, what I still recall most vividly of the adventure is singing Pamplona songs in the packed town square, surrounded by 20,000 other like-minded people with a girlfriend by my side, a bullfight and a bull run to come and thinking, almost aloud: "At last, at long, long last I am alive; and all those fools, who told me that their school years were the best years of their life, must have either had a much more exciting school career than I had endured, or more likely have had a damned dreary life since!"

However, had it not been for those photographs in *Death in the Afternoon* I would never have been there at all. What photographs they are. On the first page is a photo of the matador Chicuelo (passing a bull to perfection) and opposite it is captioned simply, "Chicuelo, who could do this." The next photos are captioned, "But was afraid of this" (an operation on a horn wound), "And of this" (Chato being carried severely wounded from the ring), "And of this" (Granero being killed in the Madrid Bullring), "And of this" (Granero in the mortuary, surrounded by people, only two of whom are looking at the dead man, the rest concerned only with how they will look in the photograph), "And of this" (the magnificent bull that Vicente Martinez could not kill).

It was these photographs, and those terse captions, that compelled me to learn more of the corrida and eventually to go to Pamplona, and, as a result, to discover a consuming interest that has never left me. My gratitude to the late author and those (un-credited) photographers is undying.

*

I feel certain that Amanda Lockhart and Dan Abraham's images in *The Art of the Race* will open up our sport to many people in a similar manner. Some of these images hold a haunting quality – something simple and commonplace, delineated more deftly. Others are more dramatic – the fleeting second of a race frozen, so that the longer the photographs are examined, the more is revealed.

Some readers may well come to regard the photographs in this book as their catalyst too, that leads them to derive endless pleasure from the sport, or even perhaps to fashion for themselves a career in what is still the Sport of Kings.

And for those who know it all already? If they give these photographs the scrutiny they deserve, they will know that little bit more about the intricacies of a sport that they had previously thought they knew everything about.

Stud Farms and Foaling

Previous page - Foal at the National Stud.
Left - Millennium Statue, Newmarket.

This page - *Top left* the rump of Oasis Dream, currently the most successful British stallion, who stands at Juddmonte's Banstead Manor Stud. His stud fee for 2010 was £65,000 per mare.
Top right Haafhd, winner of the 2000 Guineas in 2004, in action at Shadwell's Nunnery Stud.
Bottom left Feed-buckets at the National Stud.

This page - Two foals born in daylight and within an hour of each other at Juddmonte Farms, Wargrave.
Opposite - Mare and foal at Silfield Stud, Newmarket.

Foal at the National Stud.

Mare and foal being turned out at Juddmonte Farms, Wargrave.

Overleaf (pages 20 & 21) - Mares and foals at Juddmonte's Banstead Manor Stud, Newmarket.

Mares and foals being turned out into new pasture at Newsells Park Stud.

Banstead Manor Stud.

Early Training for
Horse and Jockey

Previous page - Yearling training at Ferrans Stud in County Meath, the Irish arm of Juddmonte Farms.
This page - Yearling fillies at Tweenhills Farm and Stud in Gloucestershire.

Yearlings being nannied by a shire horse at Coolmore Stud in Co. Tipperary.

Yearlings being walked, lunged and taken through the starting stalls at Ferrans Stud and Coolmore.

Young horses being measured and backed at Ferrans Stud.

Tattersalls sales being conducted by auctioneers Philip Myerscough (*bottom left*), Todd Watt (*bottom right*) and (*following page*) Simon Kerins.

The sales-ring at Tattersalls, Newmarket. Founded in 1776, Tattersalls is the oldest bloodstock auctioneers in the world and offers over 10,000 thoroughbred horses for sale each year. The highest priced sale to date was that of Magical Romance at the mares sales in December 2006, who was sold to Lady Serena Rothschild for a record-breaking 4.6 million guineas.

Young jockeys being put through their paces at the British Racing School in Newmarket.

All flat and jump jockeys riding under licence must attend either this school or the Northern Racing College in Doncaster to learn the basics of race-riding, starting on horse simulators. A new simulator has recently been introduced called the 'Equishoot', which for the first time will allow jockeys to learn to fall off safely. Up until now, they have had to learn the hard way.

Jockey coach and ex-professional jockey Richard Perham teaching a young jockey how to use his whip correctly.

The racehorse simulator, complete with whipping sensors, as well as sensors for the bit, saddle and neck, helps jockeys ride correctly and improve their balance, strength and fitness. The TV monitor can be programmed to give jockeys a virtual experience of any race or race-track.

Gallops and Racing Stables

This page and previous page - The Gallops at Lambourn, The Valley of the Racehorse. With over 50 racing yards and approximately 2000 horses in training, Lambourn is one of the main training centres in England. The Gallops were purchased by the Jockey Club in 2005.

A lone horse makes its way up Nicky Henderson's private gallops in Lambourn.

Over the page - Nicky Henderson walking with his string at they head back down the hill to Seven Barrows Stables.

Following pages (pages 46 and 47) - Pictures from the gallops at Lambourn, Nicky Henderson's gallops and covered open-air school and Ferdy Murphy's gallops in Leyburn, North Yorkshire.

Horses preparing for their second canter up Warren Hill in Newmarket. The Newmarket Training Grounds, owned and managed by Jockey Club Estates, comprise 50 miles of turf gallops and 14 miles of artificial track. They are used every day by over 2,500 horses under the watchful eye of around 70 different trainers.

Horses head back from the Rowley Mile gallops in Newmarket. Charles II made Newmarket fashionable for race meetings in 1622. The Rowley Mile is named after him. (Old Rowley was the name of Charles II's favourite horse, but the name later became a nickname for Charles himself).

Clockwise - Nicky Henderson overseeing final preparation for 2006 Grand National runner, Iris Royal, Sir Mark Prescott's indoor school, Alan King's outdoor school and early morning gallops on The Curragh in Co. Kildare.

Unsaddling after morning exercise at Philip Hobbs' yard in Somerset.

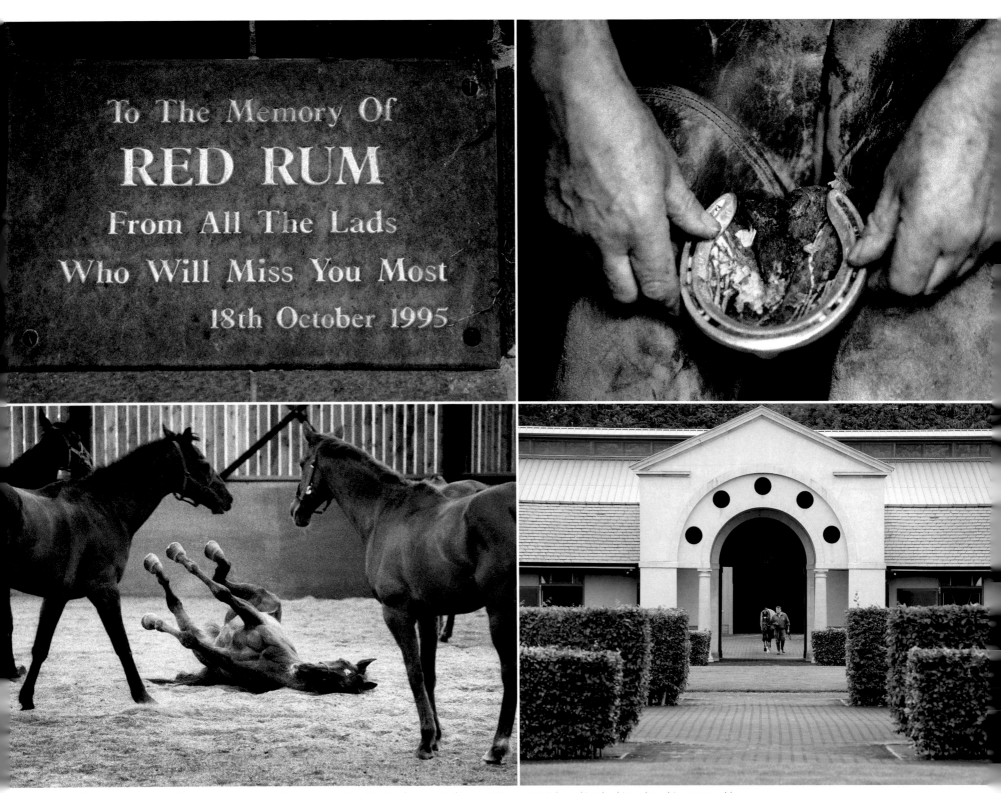

Clockwise, starting top left - A memorial plaque to three-times Grand National winner Red Rum at Ginger McCain's yard in Cheshire, where his son Donald now trains, a horse being shod, horses being led back to their stables after being taken out for a pick of grass at Ballydoyle, Co. Tipperary and horses at Ferdy Murphy's training yard are let loose for a roll in his indoor school after a morning on the gallops.

Kauto Star in his stable at Paul Nicholls' training yard in Somerset. Kauto Star is one of the greatest and most successful National Hunt horses of all time.
He has won the Cheltenham Gold Cup twice (2007 and 2009) and is the only horse to have won the King George VI Chase four consecutive times.
Over the page - R&R at Ferdy Murphy's and feeding time at Michael Bell's.

Behind the Scenes

Workers at Allertons, the leading makers of racing colours and racing silks in Europe, here making some new racing silks, and sheets for the winners of the 2007 Oaks and Derby (Light Shift and Authorized respectively as it turned out).

This page - individually labelled rolls of silk for the making of owners' colours, including, centre left, the label denoting the blue used for Mrs Sue Magnier and Coolmore Stud.

Following pages (pages 60 and 61) - Berney Bros Saddlers in Co. Wexford, one of Ireland's best-known producers of racing saddles. The firm has been run by the same family for five generations, since 1880.

Valets at Huntingdon (*top two pictures*), Newbury (*bottom left*) and Aintree (*bottom right*). Every professional jockey is assigned to a particular valet who will look after them at race-meetings. Each valet will look after approximately 12-15 jockeys. Many of them are ex-jockeys, including, *bottom left picture on the left*, Chris Maude, who now owns and runs the biggest team of valets.

Brian Alexander organising the numbers at Newmarket July Course.

Officials at Newmarket July Course (*top left*) and Ascot.

Ascot vet (*top two*) and doctor waiting for patients in the race-course hospital (*bottom left*) and the Newmarket farrier.

The Changing and
Weighing Rooms

Previous page - Ruby Walsh on Grand National Day in 2007.
Above - Jockeys in the steam room at Newbury Racecourse.

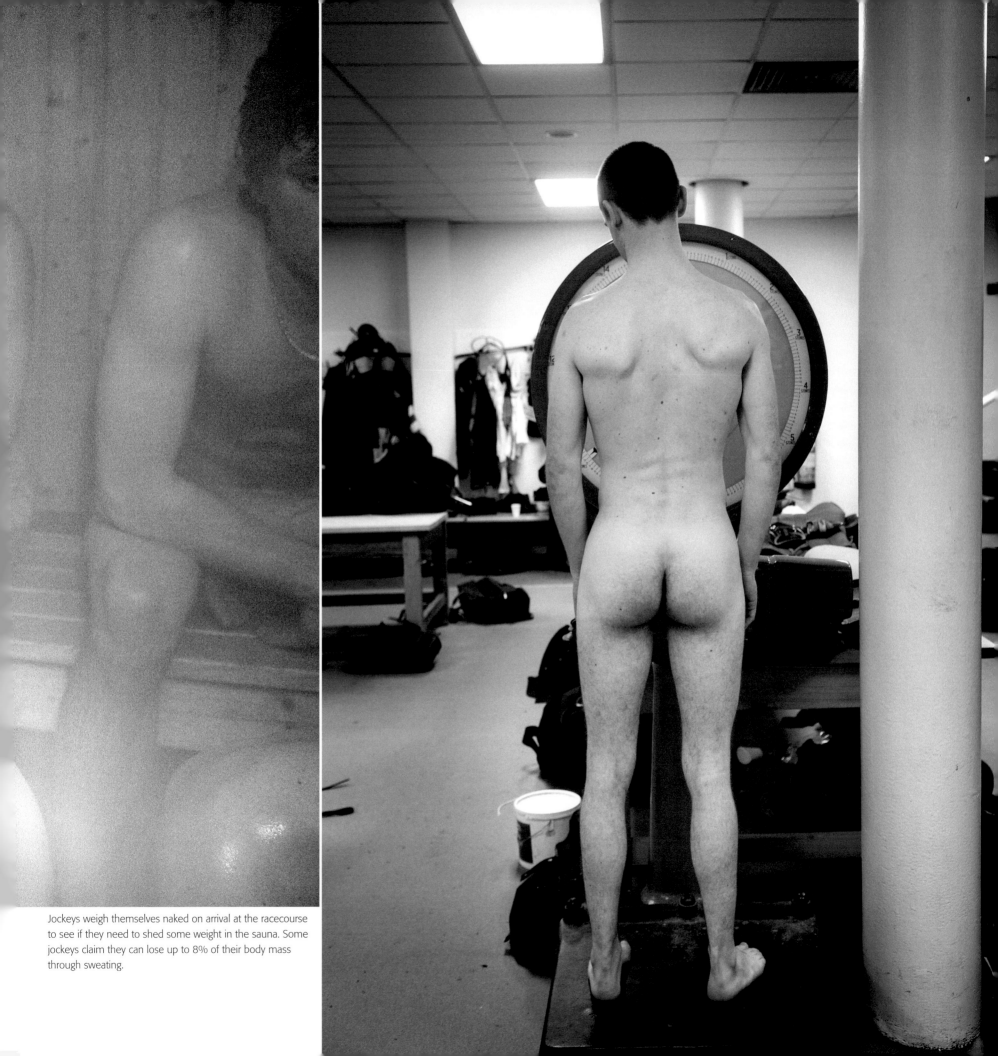

Jockeys weigh themselves naked on arrival at the racecourse to see if they need to shed some weight in the sauna. Some jockeys claim they can lose up to 8% of their body mass through sweating.

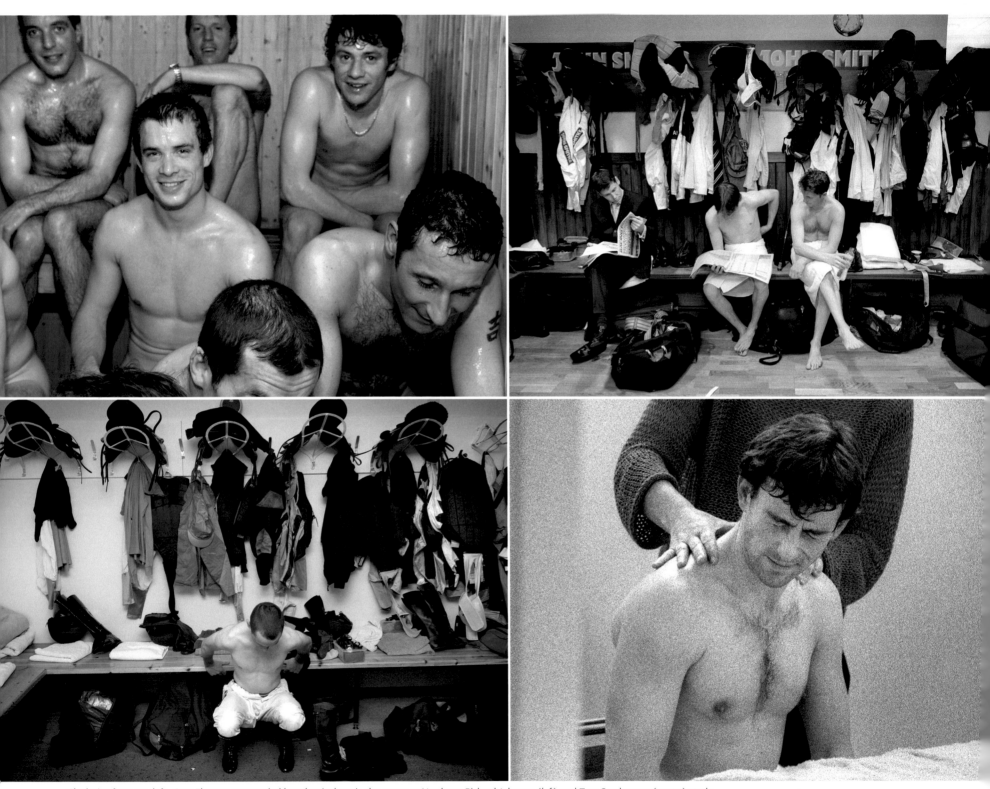

Clockwise from top left - Sam Thomas surrounded by other jockeys in the sauna at Newbury; Richard Johnson (*left*) and Tom Scudamore (*centre*) study the form at Aintree on Grand National Day, Mark Bradburne receives some attention from the physio and a jockey does some stretching at Newbury.
Opposite page - Tom Scudamore (left) and Jamie Moore watching the racing at Aintree.

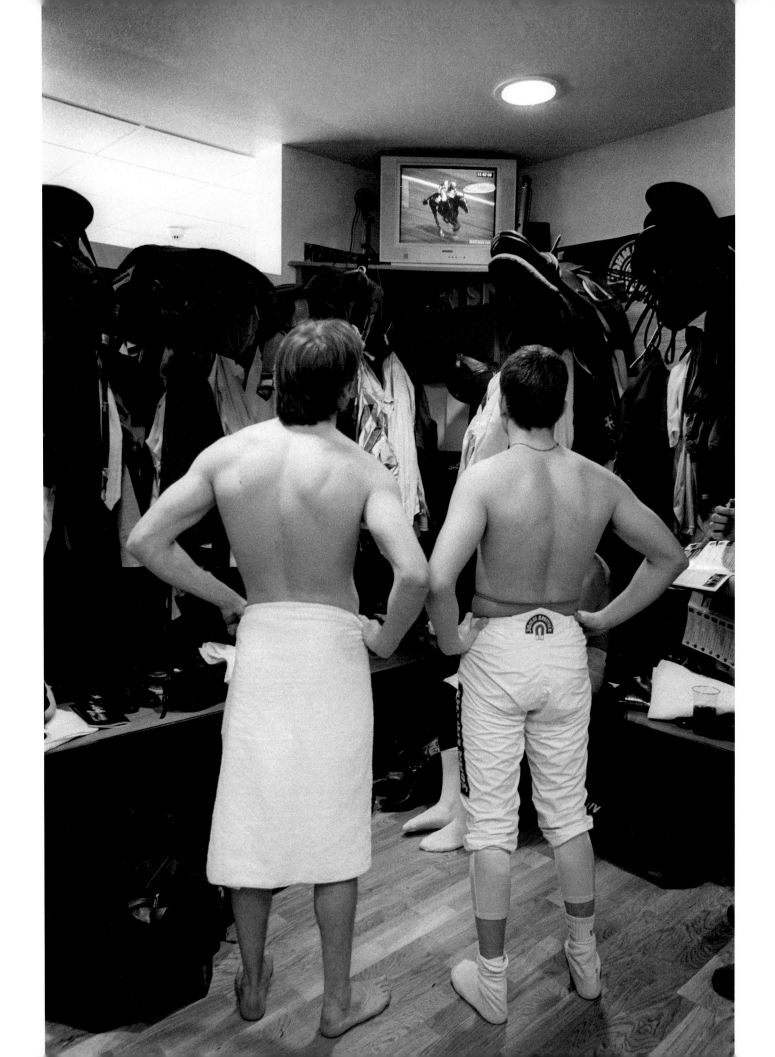

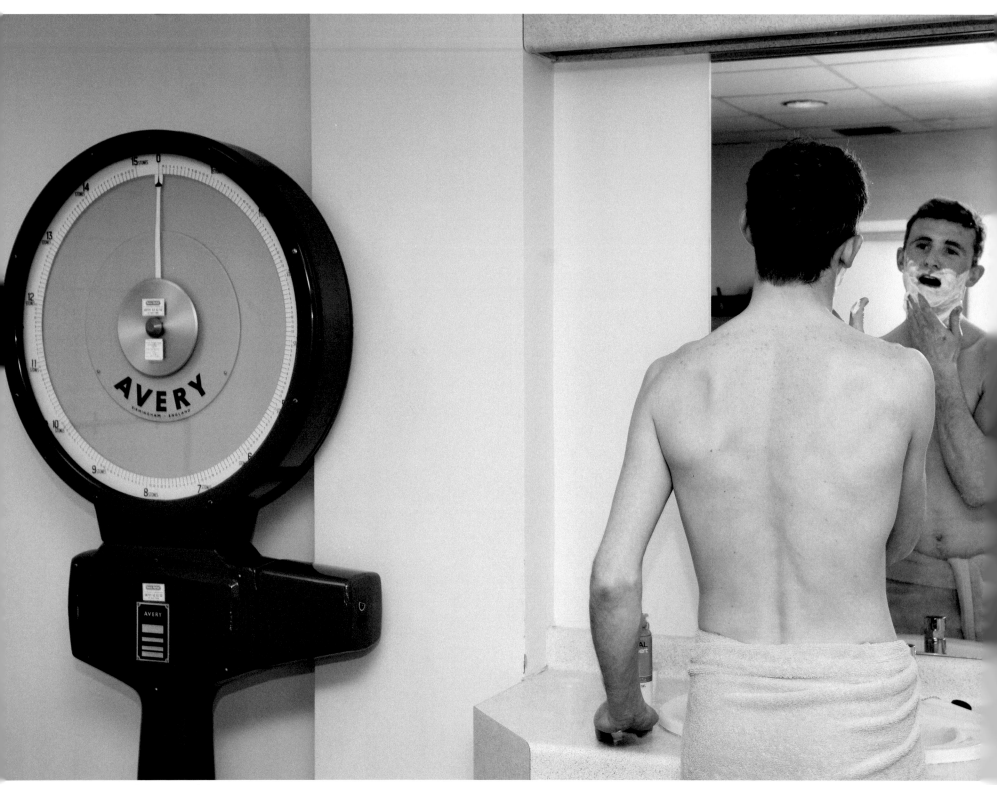

Derek Laverty shaving at Newbury.

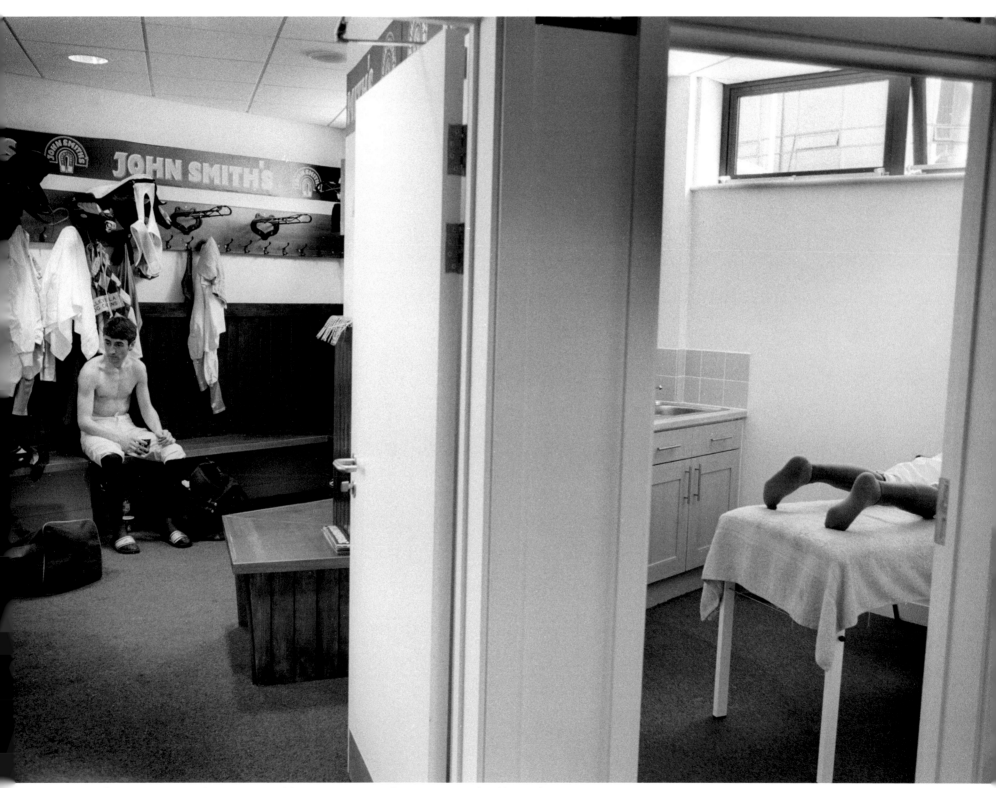

Dougie Costello waiting for racing to begin at Aintree, while AP McCoy receives physio treatment on the table next door.

Left - Jimmy McCarthy resting before racing at Newbury.
This page - The Hills twins (Richard *left* and Michael *right*) in the weighing room at Newmarket.

Clockwise from top left - Leighton Aspell being weighed out at Huntingdon, a weighing room official, Joe Fanning talking to Jamie Spencer at Newmarket and jockey Philip Hide with a trainer at Newbury.

Above - Paul Fessey (*left*) and Richard Johnson.
Following page - Master Minded, dual winner of the Queen Mother Champion Chase at Cheltenham, was the highest rated chaser in the world following the 2007/8 season.

The Paddock and
Pre-Race Preparation

John Gosden at Newmarket

William Haggas at Royal Ascot.

Ed Dunlop at the July Course in Newmarket.

Tommy Burns, one of the travelling head lads for Sheikh Mohammed's Godophin racing operation.

Aidan O'Brien with his 2009 Derby jockeys, left to right Pat Smullen, Richard Hughes, Seamus Heffernan, Johnny Murtagh, Ryan Moore, and Colm O'Donoghue.

Clockwise from top left - Nicky Henderson talking to the press, Jonjo O'Neill saddling up at Newbury, trainer François Doumen (*right*) giving some pre-race advice to jockey Barry Keniry and, bottom left, Saeed bin Suroor at the Newmarket July Course.

Aidan O'Brien saddling Alexandrova before her Epsom Oaks win in 2006. The Sadler's Wells filly went on to win both the Irish Oaks and the Yorkshire Oaks in the same year.

Henry Cecil

Richard Hannon senior and junior at Royal Ascot.

Representatives from team Coolmore at Epsom. From left to right, Timmy Hyde, John Magnier, David O'Loughlin and Richard Henry.

Michael Stoute at Ascot.

Four times Champion Owner, Sheikh Hamdan al Maktoum, in the paddock at Royal Ascot.

Sheikh Mohammed al Maktoum, the predominant figure in thoroughbred racing and breeding throughout the world, seen here at Ascot with his wife, Princess Haya. His racing interests include Darley Stud in Newmarket and the Godolphin racing operation.

Trainer Jim Bolger looking at New Approach, before the 2000 Guineas in 2008, in which he was runner-up to Henrythenavigator. New Approach, owned by Princess Haya, went on to win the 2008 Derby.

William Barlow, steward at Kempton races.

Ferdy Murphy in the saddling stables at Newbury.

Two officials at Epsom.

Left - Former jockeys Willie Carson and Ray Cochrane working for the BBC in the paddock at Royal Ascot.
This page - Sheikh Hamdan (*above left*) and Her Majesty the Queen (*bottom left*) talking to Lord and Lady Derby at Epsom, and, *top right and bottom right*, racegoers at Goodwood and Ascot.

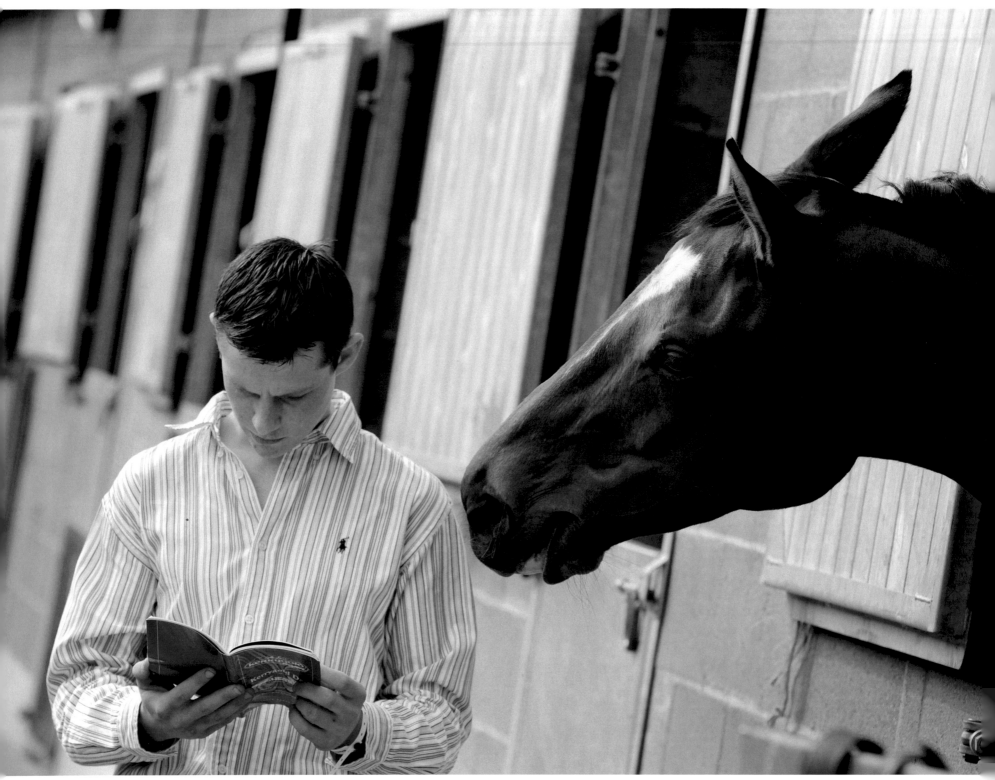

Checking the race-cards and form at Punchestown (*above*) and Ascot (*right*).

Left - Bookies at Sandown.
This page - The terrifying spectre of racing pundit John McCririck on the big screen at Cheltenham during the Gold Cup Festival.

Clockwise from top left - Crowds at Newbury (top two), Ascot and Newmarket.

Stall-handlers at Newmarket.

Left - Paddock crowd at Royal Ascot.
This page - a race-goer at Newmarket (*left*) and going down to the start of the 2007 Epsom Derby.

Previous page - Pipedreamer (number 6) with Martin Dwyer winning The Alphameric Vase at Goodwood in 2007.
Above left - Changing the stall numbers and (*right*), checking girths on the Newmarket July Course.

Clockwise from top left - The tools of the stall-handler's trade, the flagman at Newmarket, girth-tightening at Punchestown and starter Sean McDonald.

Loading up the stalls at the July Course in Newmarket.

Left - Race-goers at Cheltenham.
Above - Stewards at Newmarket July Course.

Starts at Newmarket (*above*) and Punchestown (*right*).

Setting off along the Newmarket July Course.

Mud flying at Wincanton.

The water-jump at Leicester Racecourse.

Runners in The Racing Post Chase at Kempton, 2009.

Clockwise from top left - The field and crowds at Punchestown, Robert 'Choc' Thornton flying through the air at Aintree, AP McCoy and Paddy Flood in action at Punchestown and Sam Thomas and AP McCoy matching strides at Aintree.

Ruby Walsh (on the horse nearest) easily clearing a fence at Punchestown, with AP McCoy to the left.

Beach racing at Laytown, Co. Meath.

Top left - Robbie Power in the La Touche Cup at Punchestown, sits tight on the first circuit, and (*top right*) gets it right second time round.
Bottom left - A loose horse at Punchestown and (*right*), racing at Laytown.

Jumps and falls, including Piraya and Timmy Murphy at the last fence at Ascot (*top left*).

Above - Number 8, De Luain Gorm and jockey Gordon Gallagher come to grief at The Chair in the 2009 John Smith's Foxhunter's Chase, (*top right*) a jockey struggles to stay on at Kempton and (*bottom right*) Mick Fitzgerald and his horse Crozan get trampled at Becher's Brook in the John Smith's Topham Steeplechase at Aintree, 2008. Two days later another fall on the same course, this time on L'Ami in the Grand National, put an end to Fitzgerald's racing career.

Clockwise from top left - Ruby Walsh on Celestial Halo (*left*) and AP McCoy on Binocular battle it out in the 4 year-old Novice Hurdle at Aintree, 2008, Mick Fitzgerald on Fondmort leading over the last at Cheltenham in 2006, AP McCoy falling at Aintree in 2009, and Ruby Walsh on Master Minded on his way to winning the Victor Chandler Chase, Ascot 2009.

Richard Johnson falling at The Chair in the Grand Sefton Chase, Aintree 2005.

and Celebrations

Previous page - Royston Ffrench on Laa Rayb (far side) riding it out against Darryll Holland on Stimulation in the first race on Champions' Day at Newmarket in 2008.

Clockwise from top left - Fleeting Spirit and Tom Queally winning the Darley July Cup, 2009, Mick Fitzgerald winning on Binocular at Kempton, Raven's Pass, the first English trained winner of the Breeders' Cup Classic, seen here at Newmarket, and Sheikh Hamdan's Awzaan with Richard Hills winning the Middle Park Stakes at Newmarket in 2009.

Action from Longchamp in 2007.

Richard Hughes, crossing the finishing line, Newmarket July Cup day, 2008.

Spectators at Cheltenham watch the racing live and on the big screen.

Three noses at Newmarket.

Sea the Stars, one of the greatest flat race-horses to date; winner in 2009 of the 2,000 Guineas, the Derby, the Eclipse, the International Stakes, the Irish Champion Stakes and the Prix de l'Arc de Triomph, before retiring to stud at the age of 3. Here with Mick Kinane winning the Arc at Longchamp.

Henrythenavigator (*left*) ridden by Johnny Murtagh edges past New Approach in the 2000 Guineas in 2008.

The face of victory. *Clockwise from top left* - Three Juddmonte winners: Maxime Guyon on Byword wins the Prince of Wales's Stakes at Royal Ascot, 2010, Tom Queally on Twice Over wins the Champion Stakes at Newmarket, 2009, and Stephan Pasquier on Special Duty (*left*) wins the 1000 Guineas after a stewards' enquiry, 2010. *Bottom left:* Kieren Fallon on Strike the Deal winning the Scarborough Stakes, 2009.

Davy Bonilla on Naaqoos winning at Longchamp, 2008.

Ruby Walsh and trainer Paul Nicholls celebrate Kauto Star's Cheltenham Gold Cup win in 2009.

Don't Push It gives AP McCoy his first Grand National win in 15 attempts, 2010.

Denis O'Regan and Inglis Drever win the World Hurdle at Cheltenham 2008.

Paddy Brennan triumphant after winning the 2010 Cheltenham Gold Cup on Imperial Commander.

Left - Olivier Peslier at Ascot, after winning the King's Stand Stakes on Equiano in 2008.
This page - Frankie Dettori celebrates winning the Derby, after 14 previous unsuccessful attempts, on Authorized in 2007 and
(*bottom right*) squirting the crowds with champagne at the Newmarket July Course.

Clockwise from top left - Jockey Frederik Tylicki with his Champion Apprentice Jockey Trophy being showered in champagne, Johnny Murtagh celebrates riding Yeats to his record-breaking fourth Gold Cup win at Royal Ascot, Mick Fitzgerald after winning the Tingle Creek on Kauto Star. Bottom left: Forpadydeplasterer and Barry Geraghty with The Goat Racing Syndicate celebrating after winning The Arkle at Cheltenham, 2009.

AP McCoy celebrates his 2010 Grand National win on JP McManus's Don't Push It after being handed the trophy by comedian Peter Kay (left).

The also-rans - Jockeys Jason Maguire and Andrew Tinkler after a race at Cheltenham and (*right*) Simon Whitworth at an evening meeting at Kempton.

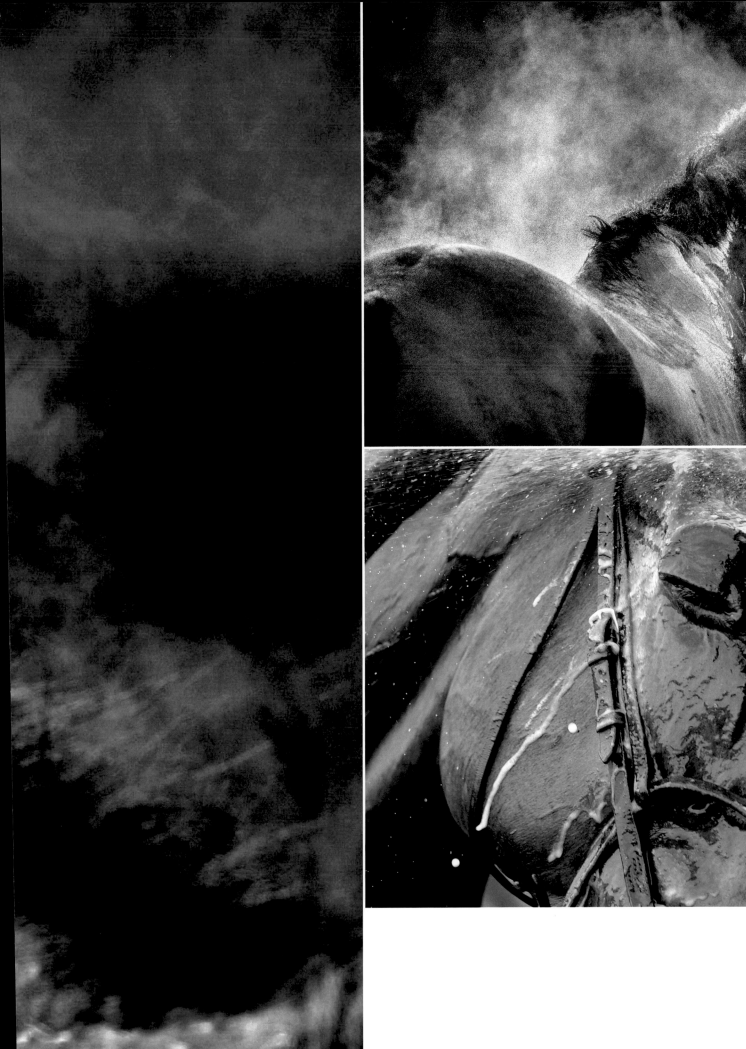

Cooling off after racing at Aintree (*left*), Newmarket July Course (*right*) and Warwick (*far right*).

Heading back to the stables at Taunton.
Following page - Frankie Dettori in the starting stalls at Newmarket.

The Portraits

Martin Dwyer
Hayley Turner
Kieren Fallon
William Buick

Lester Piggott and Frankie Dettori
Jimmy Fortune
Johnny Murtagh
Richard Hughes

Kevin Manning
Paul Hanagan
Frankie Dettori
Ryan Moore

Seb Sanders
Jamie Spencer
Eddie Ahern
Darryll Holland

Ruby Walsh	Nina Carberry	Richard Johnson	Timmy Murphy
Paddy Brennan	Sam Thomas	Mattie Batchelor	Jason Maguire
Denis O'Regan	Robert Thornton	Andrew Thornton	Aidan Coleman
Barry Geraghty	AP McCoy	Graham Lee	Tom Scudamore

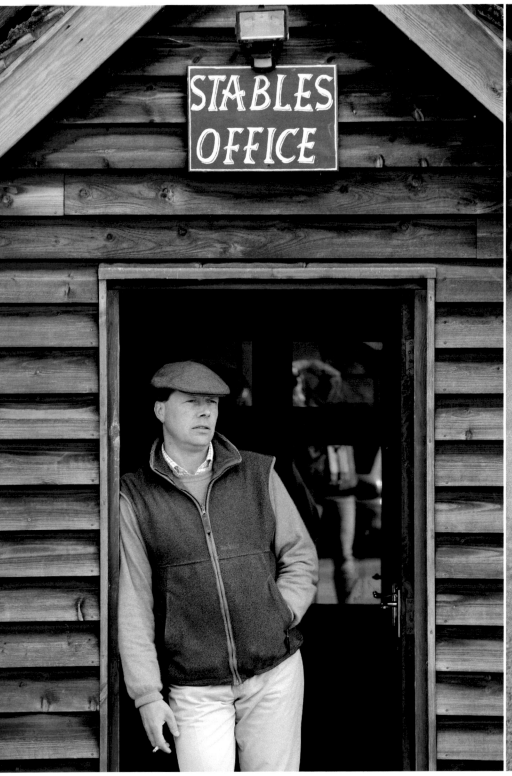

Henry Daly.

Martin Pipe.

Denman.

Philip Hobbs.

Vincent O'Brien
Brian Meehan
Aidan O'Brien
David Elsworth

Barry Hills
Ed Dunlop
Andrew Balding
Michael Bell

John Dunlop
Henry Cecil
Jeremy Noseda
Marcus Tregoning

Mark Johnston
Luca Cumani
Michael Stoute
Saeed bin Suroor

Charlie Mann
Venetia Williams
Martin Pipe
Oliver Sherwood

Brendan Powell
Ferdy Murphy
Howard Johnson
Paul Nicholls

Nicky Henderson
Ginger McCain
Jessica Harrington
Donald McCain

Alan King
Willie Mullins
Nigel Twiston-Davies
Henrietta Knight

Clare Balding.

Sir Peter O'Sullevan.

Adrian Camm.

John Francome.

Harry Herbert
Lord Daresbury
Princess Haya
Julian Richmond-Watson

The Duke of Roxburghe
Luke Lillingston
Lord Halifax
Prince Khalid Abdullah

Charles Barnett
Jeff Smith
Ricky Hambro and Lady De La Warr
Lord Teddy Grimthorpe

Brian O'Rourke
Simon Crisford
Eric Penser
Michael Tabor

John Maxse
Clive Smith
David Johnson
Hugh Barclay

Andy Stewart
David Redvers
Paul Barber
Henry Beeby

JP McManus
Harvey Smith
Alice Plunkett
David Minton

Harry Findlay
Marcus Armytage
Graham Wylie
Raymond Mould

Her Majesty the Queen and Prince Philip.

Kevin Darley.

Luca Cumani talking to Lord De La Warr.

Barry Hills with a friend.

DAVE DICK by Nicholas Godfrey

First published in the Independent on Wednesday, 21 February 2001

Renowned as the hardest of the hard men, Dave Dick was one of the top jump jockeys in post-war Britain and a serious contender for the greatest jump jockey never to have been champion. His swashbuckling style and colourful character ensured he stood out in the National Hunt scene in the 1950s, an era now revered as a golden age for steeplechase riders.

Despite a constant struggle with his weight - at six feet tall, he was distinctly on the large side for a jockey - Dick partnered numerous big-race winners. Among them was one of the most dramatic victories of all-time in the 1956 Grand National, where he rode ESB. The race is better known for its runner-up Devon Loch, who inexplicably collapsed when seemingly assured of victory 50 yards from the line under Dick Francis, riding for the Queen Mother. Newsreel footage of the race has become a staple of television coverage at Aintree; seldom is it mentioned that it is Dick who careers past the stricken Devon Loch.

Dick also won the Cheltenham Gold Cup - a more prestigious race to cognoscenti than the National - on Mont Tremblant as well as many other major contests, including several at jump racing's holy of holies, the National Hunt Festival.

The son of an Epsom-based trainer, Dick was born in 1924 and attended the same school as his lifelong friend Fred Winter, who was to become champion jockey and trainer, and a racing legend in the process.

Apprenticed to his father, also named Dave, Dick started as a Flat-race rider and secured his first winner at Brighton in September 1938. In 1941 he won the high-profile Lincolnshire Handicap on Gloaming. Burgeoning weight meant Flat racing was soon to be forgotten by the young rider in favour of jumping, where more mature horses are set to carry heavier burdens, but he remains the only rider to have won both halves of the so-called Spring Double, the Lincoln and the National.

Dick shot to prominence in the National Hunt world in 1951 when he was retained to ride the horses of the leading owner Dorothy Paget, who were trained by the great Fulke Walwyn and for whom he rode Mont Tremblant to Cheltenham success the following year. The victory was particularly noteworthy as the horse was technically a novice, in that he had never won over fences before the season in question, which made winning the Gold Cup an incredible feat.

Dick's weight problems - he spent countless hours attempting to shed unwanted pounds - meant he could never rely on the numerical firepower needed to become champion jockey. But he was famed as a big-race specialist, his reputation as the strongest finisher in the sport with a courageous spirit to match, combining to produce an impressive strike-rate in the top events.

Besides the "crown jewels" of the National and Gold Cup, Dick won the Two-Mile Champion Chase twice, including victory in 1965 on Dunkirk, one of the greatest two-mile specialists in racing history. He was also associated with Pas Seul, another of the Sixties' leading steeplechasers, aboard whom he won the 1961 Whitbread Gold Cup. Dick's career total of 348 jumps winners featured an unusually high quota of the sport's bigger prizes and he remained at the top of the tree for 15 years until his retirement in 1966.

By that time, his exploits and sayings had also became the stuff of legend; his close friend and former colleague Terry Biddlecombe, himself three-times champion jockey, has described Dick as "the funniest man in racing". According to the Racing Post, a typical example of Dick's wit occurred at the start of one Grand National, always a fractious time for the jockeys involved. On this occasion, a man was sighted carrying a banner which read: "Repent or your sins will find you out." Dick is reported to have given the individual a long, hard look, turned to a fellow rider and said: "If that's the case, I won't get to the first fence!"

Few of his colleagues, among whom he was deservedly popular, would have disagreed.

The weighing room was undoubtedly a lesser place for Dick's retirement, though he stayed in the sport in bloodstock roles, including managing the Wyld Court Stud for Peter de Savary and later acting as racing manager to a Kuwaiti sheikh.

In his later years he slipped out of the public eye, but the warmth of the tributes which have been carried in the racing press since his death testify to the enduring legacy of the man who truly deserved the title "the last of the cavaliers".

ACKNOWLEDGEMENTS

The pictures on the following pages are the copyright of Dan Abraham:
53, 85, 104/5, 116 and 117, 122 - top left, top right and bottom left, 123 - left, 124 - top right and bottom left, 125, 128 - top left and bottom left, 129, 133, 135 - all four, 136/7, 138 - left and right, 139 - right, 142 - top left, top right and bottom left, 143, 146. In addition, the portraits of the following: Lester Piggott and Frankie Dettori, Hayley Turner, Paul Hanagan, Jason Maguire, Willie Mullins, Howard Johnson, Donald McCain, Simon Crisford and Micheal Tabor.

First published in Great Britain 2010
by Envisage Books
38 Wentworth Road
London
NW11 0RL
www.envisagebooks.co.uk

A catalogue record for this book is available from the British Library

ISBN 978-0-9564764-6-3

The Art of the Race designed by Nick Otway @ Alphaforme

Printed and bound by DeckersSnoeck, Belgium

Endpaper illustrations reproduced by kind permission of Allertons.com

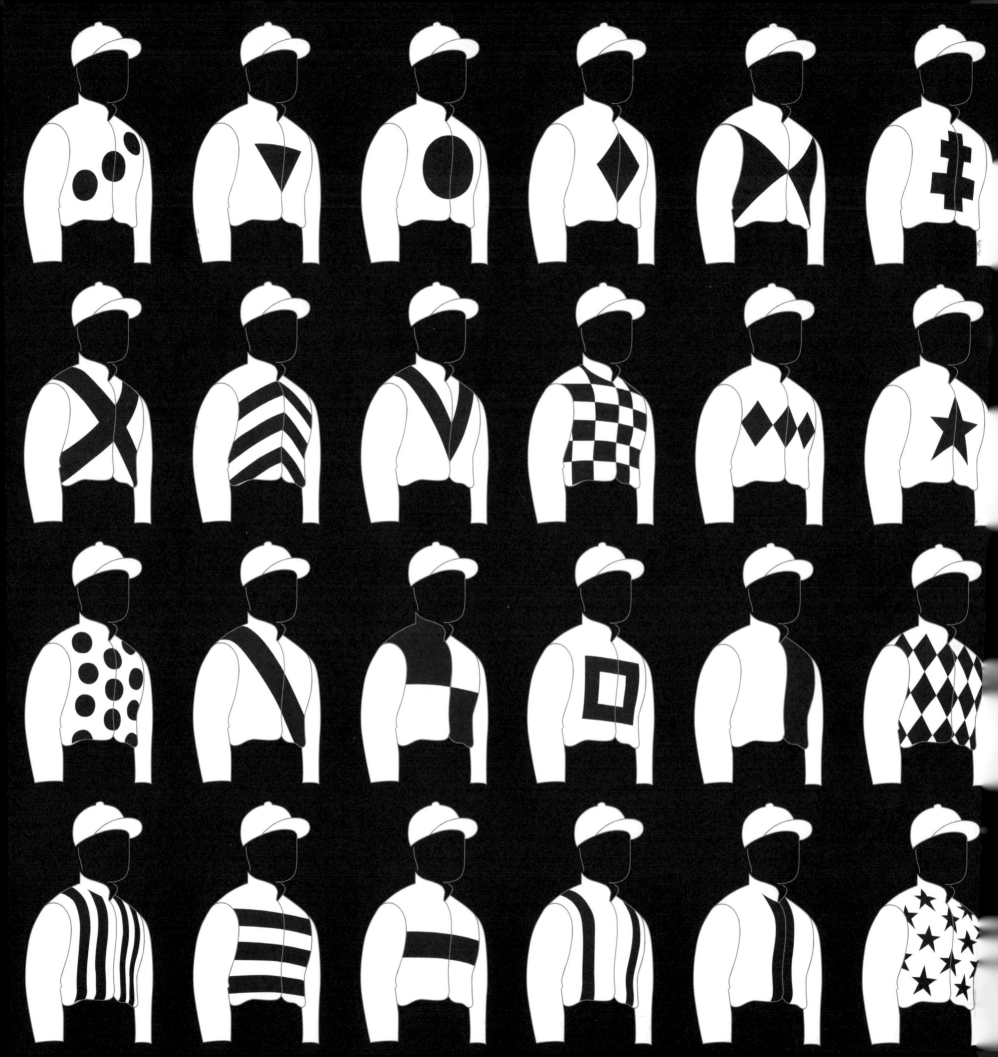